Seven Wonders of the World

By

Nick Pease

Columbus, OH

Photos: 8, © Karen SU/Corbis; **12,** © Jon Sparks/Corbis; **18,** © Bob Krist/Corbis; **23,** © Atlantide Phototravel/Corbis; **27,** © Yann Arthus-Bertrand/Corbis.

Illustrations: Carlotta Tormey

SRAonline.com

Send all inquiries to this address:
SRA/McGraw-Hill
4400 Easton Commons
Columbus, OH 43219

Printed in the United States of America.

ISBN: 978-0-07-611286-9
MHID: 0-07-611286-1

4 5 6 7 8 9 MAL 13 12 11 10 09

The McGraw-Hill Companies

Contents

—Chapter 1—

Wonders of Long Ago

*Long ago people made wonderful works of art and big buildings. People call them the "Seven Wonders of the World." Today six of the seven wonders are gone. But they are still a big part of us. Let's take a look at the Seven Wonders of the World.

1. The Great Pyramid of Giza was made about 2500 B.C. It was a tomb for a king of Egypt. Workers piled up more than two million stone blocks. Some of the blocks were nine tons! It is the oldest wonder. And* it is the only wonder left.

2. The Hanging Gardens of Babylon were on the roofs of houses. Trees and flowers were planted all over them, but without any dirt. Streams were made in the walls to water the plants.

3. The Statue of Zeus was nearly 40 feet high. Zeus was one of the Greek gods. Gold and gems covered the statue. It was made about 450 B.C.

4. The Temple of Artemis was made for a Greek goddess. The temple was over 300 feet long. The builder was King Croesus, the richest man of his time.

5. The Mausoleum at Halicarnassus held the body of a Greek king. The mausoleum was 100 feet long on each side. It held statues made by the finest artists. It was made around 350 B.C.

6. The Colossus of Rhodes was a big statue of the Greek sun god. It was over 100 feet high! It took 12 years to build.

7. The Pharos of Alexandria was a big lighthouse in Egypt. At night, sailors would see a fire on its top. This told them to keep away from the rocky shore.

Over the years, most of the wonders were broken or burned. But many new wonders were made. Are they as wonderful?

4

—Chapter 2—

The Great Wall of China

Long ago, China had many enemies. Towns made high walls to keep the enemies out. But the enemies still got in. Then, around 220 B.C., the emperor of China came up with a plan. He would build a wall from one end of China to the other.

The army got workers to build the wall. The job was very hard. Men carried stones on their backs for miles. They worked in heat, rain, and snow.

*The wall went up high hills, across rushing streams, and through wet swamps. There were few towns along the way. The work went on for hundreds of years.

The wall had big stones on the outside and rocks or sand inside. On top were towers to hide behind. There was a wide footpath on top so the army could patrol the wall. If anyone saw an enemy, he would light a fire on a tower. Armed men would come running when they saw the fire. Later the wall was lined* with cannons.

By the early 1600s all of China was walled off. At over 4,000 miles long, this was the longest wall ever made.

The Great Wall lasted many years. But keeping it in good shape took lots of money and workers. Many people were tired of it. Parts of China started fighting one another. No one tended the wall. Enemies started getting through. By the late 1600s parts of the wall were falling down.

The Great Wall kept the people of China safe for a long time. Today most of the wall is still standing. People can go and see what is left of this great wonder.

The Great Wall of China

—Chapter 3—

Petra and Angkor Wat

Lost and Found

Do you think a city could become lost?

Petra began in the Middle East around 500 B.C. It was in the wide desert of Nabatea. In those days traders passed through the desert. After many days on the road, they needed somewhere to rest and eat. It was a good spot for a town.

The name *Petra* means “rock.” It is a good name, because Petra was carved out of rock. On the side of a mountain, the Nabateans found a rock called sandstone. From it they made homes, shops, and great temples.

Traders stopping at Petra had to pay taxes on their goods. Many traders carried things from India and China to sell in Egypt and Greece. Petra made a lot of money. It became a city of more than 20,000 people.

*How could so many people live in the desert? The Nabateans were very smart. They made dams and pipes to bring water from the mountain. There was lots of water for growing food and for drinking. Better still, Petra was safe. The only way to Petra was through a small opening between two high walls. No army could rush through.

All went well until the Roman Empire took over around A.D. 100. The Romans made fine roads everywhere. Traders stopped using the Petra road. Their tax money went with them.* Everyone left the city. After hundreds of years, people forgot it was there.

Buildings in the ancient city of Petra
were carved into the side of a mountain

In 1812 a man from Switzerland got word of a "lost" city in Jordan. He went to look. He couldn't believe what he saw. Petra was almost like new. The high rock wall had kept the wind and sand away. The fine building fronts were as wonderful as ever. The lost city was found!

A Kingdom No More

In the hot jungles of Cambodia there is a grand city named Angkor. It had been the home of a great kingdom. Now it is home to monkeys and rats. Angkor was built around A.D. 1140. Miles of jungle were cleared for homes, streets, and big temples.

The work took 30 years. The people of Angkor loved the king who built their city. When he died in A.D. 1431, they built a big temple called Angkor Wat for his tomb. It was the biggest temple in the city.

Angkor Wat was a sight to see. It had fantastic statues and other works of art. Nearby, friezes hundreds of yards long were made. They had pictures of gods on them.

Soon after the king died, Angkor fell to enemies. The people escaped into the jungle. Now the once great city lies silent.

—Chapter 4—

The Taj Mahal

Most kings long ago made buildings for their own glory. In India stands the Taj Mahal, which many call the most beautiful building ever made. But it wasn't made for glory. A king made it for the woman he loved.

Shah Jahan married his wife in A.D. 1612. They were married 18 years and had 14 children. But in A.D. 1630 she died. Shah Jahan was very sad. He wanted to make the most wonderful tomb on Earth for her.

*Shah Jahan called all the best workers to his city of Agra. Masters of planning, building, and art came to the site. They stayed for years. They made a gateway, a garden, a temple, a rest house, and the Taj Mahal.

Millions have come to see the lovely grounds, the shapely dome, and the many painted pictures of plants and flowers. Money was nothing to the sad king. If something would make the building more wonderful, he wanted it. Some parts of the Taj Mahal are no bigger than a* stamp, but still have more than 50 gems on them.

But the Taj Mahal is not just a place of riches. It is a shrine to the king's love.

The Taj Mahal in India

—Chapter 5—

Nazca and Easter Island

The Lines of Nazca

Could spaceships have landed on Earth? That's what some people asked when they saw the lines and pictures on the ground in Peru.

The odd story began in 1922. People in a dry, remote part of Peru saw long lines on the ground. They seemed to form pictures. But the pictures were so big that it was hard to tell what they were.

*In 1941 a man flew over that part of Peru in an airplane. What he saw stunned him. On the ground were shapes of animals and other things. There were also big lines miles long. What could they mean?

About 70 pictures of animals were made in the earth. There was a 360-foot-long monkey, a 150-foot-long spider, and others. They were made by the Nazca people. On the flat, dry ground they had placed millions of small rocks to form the pictures. They did all of this about 2,000 years* ago.

There were also long lines of rocks that didn't form animal shapes. They couldn't be seen well on the ground, but from the air they were clear. Why are they there? To some they look like landing strips for airplanes.

But the Nazcas lived long before airplanes were made. Was this an airport for people from space?

Few believe such a fantastic idea. Still, no one has come up with a better one. That's what makes the Nazca pictures a wonder.

Easter Island

The statues on Easter Island are like nothing else on Earth. They stand as high as 40 feet. Some are over 15 tons. Hundreds of them ring the tiny island in the Pacific Ocean.

People began making the huge statues about 1,500 years ago. The workers made the statues right on the island's rock walls. With stone picks, they carved the long bodies and heads. Then they moved them to big, flat sites.

Mysterious statues stand on Easter Island

The workers had no wheels or wagons. All they had were ropes and big wooden sticks. Once they reached the flat sites, they set the statues upright. Then they lifted a big stone to the top of each statue.

They added white coral and dark stones to the statues. This made it look like they had eyes. Over time most of the stones fell out, leaving the faces dark.

What do these statues stand for? Do they stand for the bodies of kings that lie under the sites? We may never know.

—Chapter 6—

Brasilia—A Wonder?

In the late 1950s Brazil wanted to build a new capital city. They wanted it in the middle of the country. This was deep in a jungle, far from anywhere else. It would be safe from enemies. They decided to name it Brasilia.

*First, workers made an airplane landing strip and started flying in tools and food. Then, they started making roads. Brasilia began taking shape. Streets were made. Sleek buildings went up. A huge lake was dug and filled with water.

Thousands of miles of highways linked Brasilia to the rest of Brazil. In 1960 the city opened.

At first everything looked wonderful. But then things began to go bad. It took a lot of money to take care of the city. The ground was so soft that the streets and sidewalks* cracked. In the damp jungle air, green mold formed on the new white buildings. The lake became dirty. The new highways and cars were bad for the plants and animals in the jungle.

Brasilia, Brazil

Today Brasilia still has a hard time. Many like its fine buildings. But others say Brazil should have planned better. They believe the city was a mistake. What do you think?